I am, I am, I am.

This Journal Belongs To:

IF FOUND PLEASE CONTACT:

Date Began:

Date Completed:

_____

_____

_____

_____

_____

_____

_____

_____

_____

_____

_____

_____

_____

_____

_____

_____

_____

_____

_____

_____

_____

_____

_____

_____

_____

_____

_____

_____

_____

_____

_____

_____

_____

_____

_____

_____

_____

_____

_____

_____

_____

_____

_____

_____

_____

_____

_____

_____

_____

_____

SYLVIA PLATH:
A BLANK JOURNAL

Two Sylvias Press
Journalette Series

www.twosylviaspress.com

ISBN-13: 978-0692663448
ISBN-10: 0692663444

Fabric Art for Cover: Roni Johnson

because great writing
is good for the world

53792618R00048

Made in the USA
Charleston, SC
20 March 2016